SharePoint 2013 Preview – First Look

Introduction

In the Microsoft SharePoint Server ecosystem, SharePoint 2010 has been received as a solid release. In comparison to the previous release of SharePoint 2007, SharePoint 2010 provided a cleaner and easier to work with interface. Much of the cumbersome ways of managing pages, documents and lists were taken care of (at least for the most part). The introduction of the Ribbon was one of the biggest stories in that release which made the experience similar to working with the Microsoft Office client applications.

SharePoint 2013 builds upon the successful SharePoint 2010 release and further focuses on providing the user an easy to work with environment. After all, it's all about the end user when it all comes down to it, isn't it? The definition of the end user in SharePoint is not how we generally think of end users. In fact, the end user has more power and control than they are used to in the past. I define the SharePoint end user as belonging to one of the following roles:

- An owner of a SharePoint subsite

- A member/contributor of a SharePoint site

- A visitor/reader of a SharePoint site

Most people agree with this definition of the end user. Without adoption from the end users, no SharePoint initiative can be successful. That's a long standing fact! A user needs to feel that a software makes her job easier and not harder for her to really buy into and use that software effectively. What you will read about in this book is how SharePoint 2013 caters to and engages these end users. Only time will tell how successful SharePoint 2013 is in real business scenarios.

Author's note

As the author of the book, I'm Very interested in your feedback and thoughts. If you find this book helpful, please let me know! Alternatively, if you have suggestions of ways to make the book better, I'm eager to hear that too.

Best regards,

Asif Rehmani, SharePoint MVP

SharePoint-Videos.com
asif@sharepointElearning.com

Supplemental video training option

There is a whole lot of supplemental training available on the website SharePoint-Videos.com where you will find tutorials on SharePoint 2013, SharePoint 2010 and even SharePoint 2007.

Purchase of this book entitles you to 1 free month of access to all of the videos at the SharePoint-Videos.com site. Please email mailto:books@sharepointelearning.com with the proof of purchase and you will be setup with your free 1 month access to the site.

Who this Book is for

This book's target audience is the Power User of SharePoint. A power user is a person who is more advanced and empowered than an end user, but is not a hardcore developer or an IT administrator. This is the person that has a good amount of knowledge on practically working with SharePoint and helping out other users as needed by provisioning and setting up their sites for them. Having said that, end users, developers and IT professionals can also greatly benefit from the knowledge in this book to prepare themselves for what's coming in the next version of SharePoint.

This book is designed to be a very practical guide to start your learning about the specifics of what you need to know in SharePoint 2013 as a Power User. The focus is on Team Sites - not Publishing Sites - and specifically the visual elements of the sites.

What this Book is Not

- This book is not a comprehensive manual of all the changes/enhancements in SharePoint 2013

- It is not for IT professionals trying to understand the hardware/software requirements for SharePoint 2013

- It is not for developers looking to understand the SharePoint 2013 object model and development opportunities

- It is not a book on theory or abstract concepts in SharePoint. Neither will it teach you about patterns and best practices

If you keep the above points in mind as you read this book, you will enjoy it a whole lot more.

How this Book is structured

Each section of the book stands on its own. You can read the whole book in sequence or feel free to jump straight to the section that interests you most. The topics do not build on each other.

There is a heavy emphasis on visuals in this book - lots of embedded images and also video content. This book is read best on an ereader that supports images and videos.

A variety of tips and notes are peppered throughout this book in a tipbox like this one. Don't skip these. There is some very relevant info in these that you will need to know (much like the one in the following tip box)

Important: The videos and images in this book are taken from either an in-house SharePoint 2013 installation or an Office 365 preview site (SharePoint Online). They are both basically running the same SharePoint 2013 environment and are visually the same. If there are any differences in functionality that you should expect between the two environments, it is pointed out. Otherwise, you should assume that all functionality talked about in this book applies to both the on-premise installation and Office 365 (SharePoint Online).

Exploring a SharePoint 2013 site

Let's dive right in by first visualizing the SharePoint 2013 Team Site. Here it is:

SharePoint 2013 Team Site

1 The first thing that catches the eye is the boxed icons in the middle. These are created keeping the <u>Metro style</u> in mind that Microsoft is now using in every facet of their various products. It's a simple yet stylish design that you will find in Windows 8, Xbox, Windows Phone, and even <u>Microsoft's web site</u>. The icons on this team site are simply shortcuts to various 'Getting Started' actions such as setting up security, adding lists and libraries, changing site's theme etc. These shortcuts are meant to be used by the site owner to guide her through the process of setting up the site – very much like the textual 'Getting Started' links we had in SharePoint 2010 team site. Once done, these are meant to be hidden (hence the words HIDE THIS above it) before the site goes live.

2 SharePoint Ribbon resides at the top left of the site. Nothing has changed here aesthetically in comparison to SharePoint 2010. The ribbon is still the ribbon with all its coolness in-tact. Inside the ribbon, you will find some new buttons and functionality depending on the context you are in, but we are not going to dive into that here.

3 Below the ribbon, you see the new site icon with the blue background and the three partially human looking figures in white. This icon can easily be changed through *Site Settings* as in previous versions of SharePoint. Underneath that is the good old *Quick Launch* displayed in the navigation pane. This definitely looks different than what we are used in SharePoint 2010 because it has a lot fewer links. However, it works the same way and provides quick shortcut links to take users where they need to go. The *Newsfeed* link catches the eye because it's a brand new functionality. This link takes you to the newsfeed for the site – basically the activities generated by the users of the site such as adding a new document or list item, creating a page etc. It is a real handy functionality to have to keep abreast of the activities on the site. Also, notice the addition of EDIT LINKS. This is definitely new functionality which lets you, the site owner, edit the links in the quick launch quickly and easily. It is definitely much better for the site owner than having to dig into the site administration screens to find where these links are managed.

4 The top links bar on the site appears right above the title for the site. The functionality here remains the same as in the previous versions of SharePoint. The links here are perfect ways to guide the users from one site to another. Generally, you will end up putting the links to the subsites here so users can navigate to them quickly and easily. The one change here is the addition of the EDIT LINKS. Just like in the quick launch, this functionality lets the site owner quickly decide what links to expose to the site users.

5 On the top right of the page are the quick links that help with management of the site. First, there is a link to SHARE site access with users – site security management. A thorough discussion of this very important functionality appears in the next chapter. Next, there is a SYNC link. This functionality invites the site user to download and synchronize the site data on his local computer. This is accomplished using an application called Microsoft SharePoint Workspace. Workspace gets installed automatically once you install any Microsoft Office application (such as Word, Excel, PowerPoint etc) on your computer. This application is a requirement if you want to synchronize SharePoint site data on your computer. The next link is EDIT. This one is simply used to edit the page content. The one after this is the FOLLOW link. This one is a bit hard to explain quickly. Following something or someone is a new functionality baked into SharePoint 2013 which keeps you informed of any new happenings with that person or thing. A deeper discussion of this functionality appears in a later chapter (SharePoint Social) in this book.

Each of the following chapters focus on a specific facet of the new SharePoint 2013 team site. You are welcome to read them synchronously or jump directly to the one that interests you most.

Security Management of SharePoint Sites

Until now, security management of SharePoint sites in SharePoint 2010 has been a bit 'klugy'. It leaves a lot to be desired by both the users and the administrators. Requesting access to a resource or granting access to a resource should not be confusing. In fact, managing security for a site is one of the most fundamental aspects of SharePoint and should be easy and straightforward so you can move on to more pressing things that require your attention.

Following are few of the security administration challenges in SharePoint 2010:

- When site owners are granting rights to other users, they don't fully understand which permission level to grant them
- Once a site owner adds a person to a SharePoint group, they generally don't know the rights they are granting that person by performing that action
- There is no simple way to figure out who currently has access to a site
- Once an access request gets submitted by a user, it disappears into oblivion. There is no way to find out the status of that request (aside from emailing or calling the site owner)
- There is no one place where a site owner can go to manage pending access requests

The SharePoint product team set out to focus on these shortcomings and build a better sharing mechanism in SharePoint 2013 as described below.

In a SharePoint 2013 team site, when a user doesn't have access to a site and tries to navigate to it, they are presented with the request 'Let us know why you need access to this site'. Makes a lot of sense, doesn't it? It helps the user articulate why they need access when the request is sent rather than requesting the access and then having the site owner ask this question in return.

Let us know why you need access to this site.

Type your message here

Send request

Request for reasoning to gain access a site

This conversation component is visible to both the user who is requesting access and the owner(s) in charge of granting access to the site. An *Access requests and invitations* page (shown in an image at the end of this chapter) is available to the owners of the site through *Site Settings* to manage all access requests to the site. It's a great way for both parties involved to keep on top of the status of the request. The eventual result of the request and the action taken by the site owner is then archived for later reference as needed.

In many instances, a user is provided a SharePoint site and is then tasked to invite others to access the site. For this scenario, where a site owner wishes to invite folks to the site, it is a simple straightforward process. The site owner clicks the SHARE link on top left of the site and the dialog appears showing who the site is currently shared with and the fields to invite others to the site.

Inviting users to a site

Once the site owner decides who to invite and what permission level to grant them, those people get an email notifying them regarding the invitation. This process is pretty straightforward and has worked the same way in SharePoint 2010, but now has a better interface in SharePoint 2013.

How about the scenario in which someone wants to recommend that their colleague is granted access to the site? The *Grant Permissions* right is required to add someone to a site. Contributors don't have that right. So the contributors of a site can now send a request on behalf of their colleagues to have them added to the site. The process is simple. Just like a site owner, the contributor will click on the SHARE link that appears at the top right of the page. The dialog box that appears will allow the contributor to send an email invitation to the site owner with an 'on behalf of' request.

Share 'Human Resources'   ✕

👥 Shared with ☐ Irene Hernandez and ☐ Brian Cutler

Invite people

┌───┐
│ Aaron Painter x   │
│   │
└───┘

┌───┐
│ Aaron should be added to the HR site. He is part of our department. │
│   │
│   │
│   │
│   │
└───┘

HIDE OPTIONS

☑ Send an email invitation

                                        [Share]   [Cancel]

Requesting access to a site 'on behalf of' someone else

This request is then received by the site owner and can be managed just like other requests at the *Access requests and invitations* page. The message that the site owner sees is from the contributor requesting access on behalf of their colleague. The site owner can then decide with one click whether to grant access or deny it.

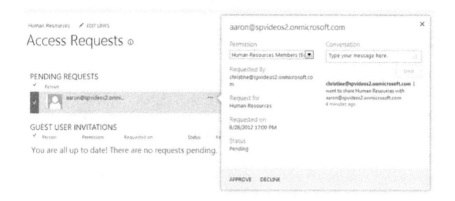

Access requests and invitations page for site owners

As you can see, a lot of pretty awesome features have been added to SharePoint 2013 , making it much easier for the site owners to manage the sharing process for their sites. With security management taken care of, site owners will be able to focus more on enhancing and managing the content of their sites.

SharePoint Branding using Themes

This chapter's focus is on site owners, designers, and power users and how they are able to customize their sites. It does not deal with creating enterprise level branding by making changes to the master page, and custom cascading style sheets (css).

Companies typically do not want their SharePoint sites to look the same as the standard SharePoint site. Individual departments in a company also may want to distinguish their departmental or project site by branding it. Typically, branding a site includes customizations of color, styles, banners, images, navigation etc. An easy way for site owners to brand their site quickly is by using SharePoint Themes. Themes represent a collection of graphics and cascading style sheets (css) that can modify how a web site looks.

In SharePoint 2010, we were able to use any of the pre-built themes or customize any of them using just the browser. If that was not enough, we were also able to use either Microsoft Word, PowerPoint or Theme Builder to create new theme files. These could then be uploaded to the theme gallery by the site collection administrator and made available for site owners and designers to use on their sites.

The whole theming engine has changed and been reworked in SharePoint 2013. Everything is based on HTML instead of any proprietary format. The image below shows the theme gallery which is filled with font and color palette files.

⊕ new document or drag files here

Themes •••

		Name		Edit	Modified
✓	🗋				
	🗋	fontscheme001	•••	🗐	Monday at 1:54 PM
	🗋	fontscheme002	•••	🗐	Monday at 1:54 PM
	🗋	fontscheme003	•••	🗐	Monday at 1:54 PM
	🗋	Palette001	•••	🗐	Monday at 1:54 PM
	🗋	Palette002	•••	🗐	Monday at 1:54 PM
	🗋	Palette003	•••	🗐	Monday at 1:54 PM
	🗋	Palette004	•••	🗐	Monday at 1:54 PM
	🗋	Palette005	•••	🗐	Monday at 1:54 PM
	🗋	Palette006	•••	🗐	Monday at 1:54 PM
	🗋	Palette007	•••	🗐	Monday at 1:54 PM
	🗋	Palette008	•••	🗐	Monday at 1:54 PM

SharePoint Themes gallery

The font (.spfont) and color palette (.spcolor) files are all completely XML based. Want to take a peak inside? Here you go:

```
fontscheme001.spfont - Notepad
File  Edit  Format  View  Help
<?xml version="1.0" encoding="utf-8"?>
<s:fontScheme name="Bodoni" previewSlot1="title" previewSlot2="body" xmlns
    <s:fontSlots>
        <s:fontSlot name="title">
            <s:latin typeface="Bodoni Book" eotsrc="/_layouts/15/fonts/Bod
            <s:ea typeface="" />
            <s:cs typeface="Segoe UI Light" />
            <s:font script="Arab" typeface="Segoe UI Light" />
            <s:font script="Deva" typeface="Nirmala UI" />
            <s:font script="Grek" typeface="Segoe UI Light" />
            <s:font script="Hang" typeface="Malgun Gothic" />
            <s:font script="Hans" typeface="Microsoft YaHei UI" />
            <s:font script="Hant" typeface="Microsoft JhengHei UI" />
            <s:font script="Hebr" typeface="Tahoma" />
            <s:font script="Hira" typeface="Meiryo UI" />
            <s:font script="Thai" typeface="Tahoma" />
            <s:font script="Armn" typeface="Segoe UI Light" />
            <s:font script="Beng" typeface="Nirmala UI" />
            <s:font script="Cher" typeface="Gadugi" />
            <s:font script="Ethi" typeface="Ebrima" />
            <s:font script="Geor" typeface="Segoe UI Light" />
            <s:font script="Gujr" typeface="Nirmala UI" />
            <s:font script="Guru" typeface="Nirmala UI" />
            <s:font script="Knda" typeface="Nirmala UI" />
            <s:font script="Khmr" typeface="Khmer UI" />
            <s:font script="Laoo" typeface="Lao UI" />
            <s:font script="Mlym" typeface="Nirmala UI" />
            <s:font script="Mymr" typeface="Myanmar Text" />
            <s:font script="Orya" typeface="Nirmala UI" />
            <s:font script="Sinh" typeface="Nirmala UI" />
            <s:font script="Syrc" typeface="Estrangelo Edessa" />
```

Font file in Theme gallery

As a result of this change in direction for theme building, you are no longer able to use Word, PowerPoint or Theme Builder to create new themes. Themes are only modifiable using the internet browser (aside from programmatic methods of course, which we will not be discussing here). Fourteen HTML 5 based themes are available out-of-the-box to be used as needed. When designing a theme in the browser, you can pick any of the provided themes as a starter template then design a much richer customized theme by choosing the fonts, color palette and your own background image.

Built-in available Theme templates

Just like SharePoint 2010 Themes, Team Sites in SharePoint 2013 do not inherit themes from their parent sites. This functionality is only available in publishing sites or in a team site with publishing feature turned on.

Aside from using packaged themes, professional designers working on enterprise branding will undoubtedly want to create their own styles using the tools they are most comfortable with. SharePoint now supports designers creating their themes using any design tool. If a designer has the skills to use HTML, CSS and javascript, she now has the skills to design for SharePoint! This topic is beyond the focus of this book. However, I would certainly encourage you to research further.

SharePoint Apps

We have all been immersed in Apps from all sorts of App marketplaces. Mobile devices, tablet computers, phones and many other major development platforms all host app marketplaces where users can go to purchase these apps. An app is basically an add-in functionality (or plug-in) that runs on top of the platform without modifying the core structure of it. In fact, one of the best aspects of apps is the decoupled natured of the apps providing flexibility for users to add and delete them without having an adverse effect on the underlying platform.

The same functionality is now being brought into SharePoint. Finally! SharePoint apps are basically self-contained pieces of functionality that extend the capabilities of a SharePoint website. This strategy has the potential of really changing the direction for the whole platform since now thousands of developers external to Microsoft will easily be able to make apps for SharePoint and make them available in the App Store. This opens up the door to truly limitless extensibility for applications of SharePoint.

Let's focus in on what this means to power users – those who are either an owner of a SharePoint site or site collection. These folks are focused on creating an appealing and easy to use environment for their users to collaborate with their peers and consume the important information made available to them on the sites. There are two types of Apps for these site owners to utilize: out-of-the-box Apps and third party Apps. Let's talk about each one briefly.

Out-of-the-box Apps

One of the main ways available for power users to build functionality within sites is with the use of list and library templates available out-of-the-box. Templates such as Announcements, Contacts, Tasks, Document Library and more are available to be used to instantiate the needed functionality to build the solution. These list and library templates are all still available in SharePoint 2013, but now they are all referred to as apps. So for example, you are no longer creating a Tasks list, instead, you are creating a Tasks app. You may wonder at this time: Is there something different about these apps from the way lists and libraries used to behave in SharePoint 2010? The answer to that is No. They are the same old lists and libraries we have always been accustomed to. They are just now officially referred to as Apps.

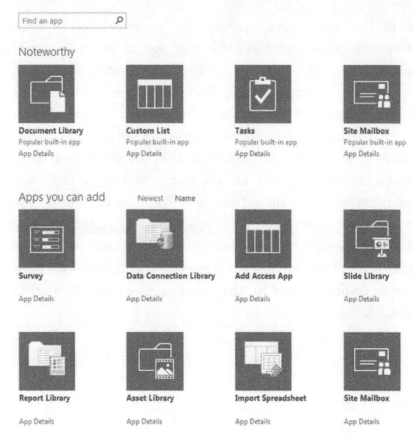

Built in App templates (formerly known as list and library templates)

Third Party Apps

Apps built by third party developers are where the actual power of the apps model will be utilized. An individual or a company can register to be an app developer for SharePoint. This provides the ability to list their custom functionality apps in the SharePoint app store, making it available to millions of people using SharePoint.

An app can be discovered and downloaded from the SharePoint app store or from an organization's private app catalog and installed at the scope of a SharePoint site. For example, let's say you have a need to create a survey to gather data. In SharePoint 2013, you can get a "survey app" from the SharePoint app store and install it on your site. Another example would be a mortgage broker who sets up a website with apps from the SharePoint store. These apps could include a "bank rates app" that helps find the best mortgage rates, a "mortgage calculator app" to help calculate mortgage payments, and a "property value estimator app" that provides an approximate value of a property.

If you are a SharePoint server administrator and are wondering how you will stop the end users from crashing your environment by introducing potentially dangerous apps, don't worry. Microsoft has provided ways to turn off access to the public app store completely from an in-house SharePoint installation so the end user cannot install an app directly. Alternatively, you, as a SharePoint server administrator, can purchase an enterprise license of an app and make that available to your users internally within the in-house SharePoint environment.

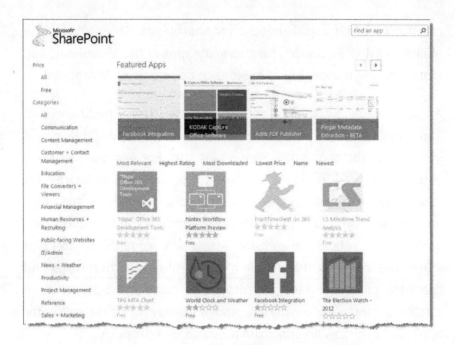

Third party Apps in the SharePoint App Store

Building third party Apps is the domain of a developer. They can use their existing skills, using familiar languages and their favorite web development tools. In addition, they can use any hosting services to run and deploy the app. Pretty cool stuff, but programming is not the focus of this book and way beyond our scope. So we'll stop talking about apps here. If you are interested in finding out more about how to build apps, I would encourage you to dive in deeper and learn how to get started <u>creating Apps for SharePoint</u>.

Managing Documents

One of the main reasons for many companies jumping on the SharePoint bandwagon has been for its document management capabilities. The words 'document management' usually bring to mind some of the following things:

- Storage of various types of documents/artifacts
- Assigning metadata for each document type
- Being able to share documents with others
- Safely viewing and editing of documents
- Moving documents from one location to another

Document libraries in team sites is the most widely used feature of a site. And, of course, you can have multiple document libraries in a site for multiple sub teams or various other document management purposes. This section will look at the major changes in how the document libraries work in SharePoint 2013 as opposed to SharePoint 2010.

Creating New Documents

When a member of a SharePoint site needs to add a document to a library, she will either be thinking of creating a new document from scratch or uploading an existing document from her computer. Let's tackle first the need to create a new document directly from the library.

First, let's quickly talk about the basic functionality from SharePoint 2010 that has not changed. Navigating to a document library page or clicking on a web part that is showing the document library brings up the ribbon. On the ribbon *Files* tab, there is a button for *New Document*. Clicking on that button opens up the default Microsoft Word document template for the library, using the Word client application installed on the computer. The user can then begin composing the document. The user can also click on the drop down arrow next to this *New Document* button and she will see all the different content types available that can be used to create the new document. None of this stuff has changed. It all remains exactly as it was in SharePoint 2010.

Now let's talk about what is new in the interface if you throw Office Web Apps in the mix. Microsoft Office Web Apps is a web based version of the Microsoft Office suite. It includes the web based versions of Microsoft Word, Excel, PowerPoint and OneNote. Which in turn means that the user does not need the Office suite on their computer. She just needs an internet browser to create and manage Office documents. A SharePoint server administrator can install Office Web Apps directly on top of an in-house SharePoint installation. Doing that will let the users create and edit Office applications directly within the web browser. When a user navigates to the library and clicks on *New Document*, they will be presented with a menu of options to create their new Office document.

Creating new documents in the library

Once again, keep in mind that this functionality is only available if you have Office Web Apps installed. Otherwise, creating new documents in SharePoint 2013 is no different than in SharePoint 2010.

Uploading Documents

The reality that I have observed, after watching hundreds of SharePoint end users over the years, is that a SharePoint user creates the document on his computer and then uploads it to SharePoint. Most users just feel more comfortable creating the documents the way they know best and then uploading them into SharePoint to share with others. There's nothing wrong with that approach.

The tough thing for these users has been the usability aspect of the upload feature in a library. You had to get used to the fact that there are two ways mainly to upload documents to a library in SharePoint 2010 when using the web interface:

1. Click on the *Add document* link at the bottom of the document library web part (not the *New Document* button in the ribbon) which brings up the dialog for browsing and selecting your document.
2. Click on the *Upload Document* button in the ribbon which brings up the same upload dialog. Through the dialog, you could choose to upload multiple documents to the library by clicking on the *Upload Multiple Files...* link.

Depending on the flavor of Microsoft Office the user is running, they would get a different experience when uploading multiple documents. Office 2007 users would have to use a windows explorer type of interface to navigate to their documents to select them for upload, Office 2010 users would get the drag and drop experience which lets you drop your files directly in the pop up window (definitely the more efficient of the two methods). The problem of course is that only folks with Office 2010 would have access to this method. In a company with a mix of 2007/2010 Office users, this made it especially challenging for the SharePoint administrators to train their users uniformly.

SharePoint 2013 makes the whole process of uploading documents much more uniform and intuitive for the end user. All they have to do is to drag the documents directly on top of the library and it takes it in. It's as simple as that. This functionality works the same when dragging entire folders from windows explorer to the library. It just absorbs it all in.

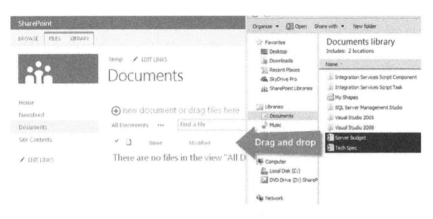

Drag and drop documents in library

Moving Documents

An important aspect of managing documents in the library is to be able to move things around within it and outside of it. This is one of the major pain points of SharePoint 2010 libraries since there are not many options for moving documents around. If you don't mind opening up the library in windows explorer and moving around documents in that view, it works fairly smoothly. However, trying to do that within the web interface doesn't get you anywhere.

This aspect of document management has improved as well in SharePoint 2013. Although, I can't honestly say that it is extremely intuitive to do so, many of the scenarios that were not possible in SharePoint 2010 have become 'do-able' in SharePoint 2013.

Here are the various scenarios for moving documents that users usually struggle with:

- From the root of the library into a folder
- From one folder into another folder
- From one library to another library

MySite Document Management

Storing personal documents in SharePoint 2013 gets a lot easier thanks to the MySite document library. Unlike SharePoint 2010, there is only one document library in SharePoint 2013's MySites (also sometimes referred to as the Mybrary).

Let me explain - SharePoint 2010 had two libraries - Shared Documents and Personal Documents. The permissions were already set for each so that the personal library was of course personal and the shared library was readable by all. This sounds nice and simple and it is. However, for a user who wants to (or has been told to) keep their documents in the MySite library, that person has to decide where to store that document at the time it's being saved. For a novice SharePoint user, this decision can get confusing at times - not knowing which library to save it to. Analysis equals paralysis in this situation and the document ends up stored on the local drive. Not a good solution.

In SharePoint 2013, there is only one document library on MySite and it's called simply Documents. When a user decides to save their documents, the documents library pops up as the default location. This makes the decision very easy for the end user as to where to store the document. In addition, there is a 'Shared with Everyone' folder (it's actually a view under the covers, but it's shown as a folder) that's in the documents library. By default, everyone in the company has read rights to that folder. The name of the folder makes it intuitive to the user to understand that any document that needs to be shared should be dropped into that folder.

A couple of default views exist in the documents library - *All* and *Shared with me*. The All view provides the overall view of documents in the documents library. The Shared with me view provides the ability to show all documents that have been shared with you across other people's My Documents libraries. It's a pretty nifty feature that relies on pre-defined search queries returning the results for you when you navigate to that view.

There is a lag between the time someone shares a document to the time it actually shows up in the Shared with me view. It can take up to 15 minutes before the document appears in your *Shared with me* view.

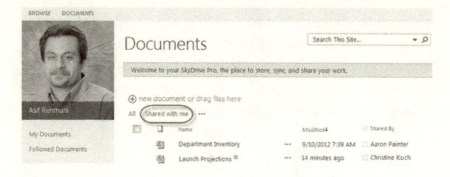

Shared with me view in Documents library

Saving documents to the 'cloud' or on a SharePoint server sounds great, because you know that it's safe and secured. However, an issue that users have always had to contend with is the unavailability of that document offline. As a user, you had to make a conscious effort to download that document to work on it and then push it back to the server when done. That extra step of remembering to save the document offline resulted in non-consistent usage of that feature. SharePoint 2013 solves that issue by allowing the user to sync their MySite documents to a local drive so that they always automatically have a local copy of their files. In the age of SkyDrive, Dropbox, Google Drive and SugarSync, this functionality to sync all your files automatically is almost expected in an enterprise collaboration system like SharePoint. Glad we finally got it!

When a user tries to save a document, let's say in Word 2013, she is presented with the following options:

1. The currently logged in SharePoint site's document library
2. The My Site documents library
3. Local computer

The first preference is to put it in the site library for all the team members of the site to see. Second choice states that if you are going to keep it as a personal document, store it 'in the cloud'. Third choice still gives them the old fashioned choice of saving it to the computer. It infers automatically then that it is a local copy and will not be shared or secured outside your computer. Of course, you want to encourage your users to choose option 1 or 2.

End users understand their files in windows explorer. Some will still prefer to store their files there no matter what. It's their comfort zone and that's understandable. Good news for SharePoint administrators - offline libraries technology powered by SkyDrive Pro ships with SharePoint 2013. What that means is that a user can get a familiar windows explorer view to interact with their documents in SharePoint 2013. This works for the documents library in MySites as well as document libraries in all SharePoint sites.

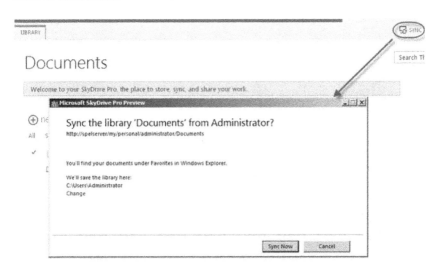

Sync library offline to your computer

To set up the offline sync, user will need to click on the SYNC button on the top right corner of the site. The user is then prompted for permission to sync that library on his computer. If the user agrees, then all documents from that library are copied <u>and</u> kept in sync with the files in the document library. Now the beauty of this process is that a user with multiple computers can perform this same step on each computer for a library to keep the documents in sync on all of his computers. The synced document has a little green checkmark, overlaying the document icon, signifying that they have been synced with the server copy. All of these documents are safely secured at the SharePoint server as well and thus in the SQL database. In addition to all that, the system tray area has the SkyDrive Pro utility running that can be used to control the sync of this library and even start syncing another library. It all truly looks and feels like Dropbox has now come to SharePoint!

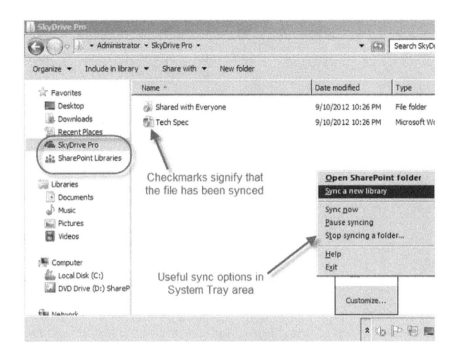

Skydrive Pro used to sync documents offline

For the offline sync functionality to work on the client machine, the user would need one of the Microsoft Office 2013 applications (such as Word, Excel, PowerPoint). Any one of them will do. The reason here is that by installing the Office client, it's installing the underlying functionality needed to make this work. Under the covers, this process is installing and configuring the good old SharePoint Workspace which in SharePoint 2013 has now been redesigned to use MySite Documents library.

The end result is that user sees the synchronized documents in the windows explorer where they are most comfortable with seeing their other documents as well. It's a win-win scenario for the user, who wants easy access and manageability of the documents, and the SharePoint administrator, whose responsibility it is to keep all documents secured and backed up.

List Management

SharePoint is entirely list driven. Almost everything is essentially a list with rows of data and columns (metadata) describing that data. Lists are a fundamental part of everything that you do within SharePoint sites. I will assume here that you have worked with lists before in SharePoint. If not, I highly recommend getting up to speed on list fundamentals and playing around with a few lists before reading further in this section.

The big question is: What has changed regarding lists in SharePoint 2013?

One big change is the way Microsoft now refers to lists in a SharePoint site. They are now officially called Apps. Chances are that most people who have been working with SharePoint for a long time will continue to refer to lists as lists instead of apps (for example, 'Tasks list' instead of 'Tasks app') and reserve the word Apps for the third party based functionality that can now be added to SharePoint 2013. To learn further about Apps in general, refer to the SharePoint Apps chapter in this book.

Quick Edit

Aside from the official name change, the truly biggest story in SharePoint 2013 with regards to lists is the addition of Quick Edit.

In SharePoint 2010 (and before that in 2007), there exists the Datasheet view. This view allows you to make changes to list data in an Excel type view. Many of us have been used to it and spoiled by it for a long time. However, it's not perfect. First of all, it doesn't work for all types of lists. A picture library, for example, does not officially support changing metadata with the datasheet view (although there are workarounds). Second, it is based upon ActiveX technology which limits you to using only Internet Explorer. Well, the reality is that there are many popular browsers out there now including FireFox, Chrome and Safari which people use on a daily basis. Forcing them to use Internet Explorer is not a popular decision.

Datasheet view is out the door and in SharePoint 2013, the quick edit view enters the scene. This view provides the same type of quick edit functionality that we all loved in datasheet view, but without the inherent complexities and limitations. Quick edit is completely javascript based and works seamlessly across all modern browsers. The best thing about it is that the experience of using quick edit is exactly the same in all browsers. Quick edit can be used for editing list or library column metadata easily and efficiently with any browser as long as javascript support for the browser is not disabled.

But wait, there's more... through the datasheet view, we could change data in existing columns, but to create a column, we still had to navigate to the *List* tab in the ribbon. That's not the case anymore. There's a plus (+) sign that appears after the last column in the list, indicating that a new column can be created there. When you click it, it provides the option to create a column with any of the various common types (such as Text, Number, Date and Time etc.) No need to take the extra step of creating the column through the ribbon. It's all right there and very intuitive for the end user.

Quick Edit view

There's one more Huge side effect that comes out of the implementation of quick edit view: The ability to edit the Managed Metadata type of column. Of course, this is only relevant to you if you have used or planning to use the managed metadata column which is based on the Term Store implementation in SharePoint. Datasheet view in SharePoint 2010 did not support the managed metadata column. To put things in perspective, let's talk through a scenario:

Let's say you have a list with a thousand records (list items) in it. You have been told that you need to add a managed metadata column to that list and then populate that column with the appropriate information for each record on that list. Adding the column is not a problem. That can be done very quickly. However, when you come to the part about editing the column information that's relevant to each record on the list, that's where you run into the problem. Since you can't change the column info in datasheet view, you would have to click on each item one at a time to open it up in edit mode and then make the change. For the hours that it takes you to accomplish this repetitive and mundane task, you will be repeating to yourself: "Are you kidding me... there has to be a better way".

In the above scenario, the quick edit view method will save you a whole lot of time because it also supports bulk copy and paste into the managed metadata column.

Hopefully, this provides you a good perspective as to how important the quick edit view will be in the day to day operations of SharePoint user.

Tasks List/App

There are small visual changes everywhere within various lists, but the most significant change is in how the Tasks list looks and behaves.

Tasks list has been around in SharePoint since the beginning of SharePoint. Not much had changed since then and it has done a decent job so far of what it promised to do – provide a way to manage tasks in a list. However, now the tasks list is getting a bit of a facelift along with some new features.

When a new tasks list gets created, a Timeline bar shows up automatically above the list to show tasks on the timeline. This provides an elegant way to visualize the task items in the list over a given period of time. The timeline bar is also configurable through the Timeline tab that appears when you click inside of a timeline as shown in the image below.

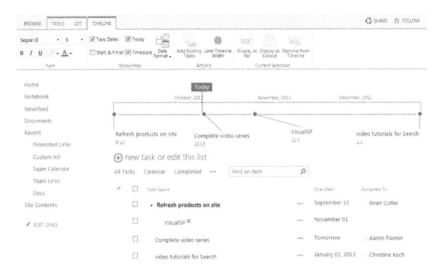

Timeline bar in the Tasks list

Another addition to the tasks list is a couple of additional pre-built views: Calendar and Gantt chart. The views themselves are not new since you can create a Calendar or Gantt chart view on any list. However, not many SharePoint users know they could instantiate these views so it has not gotten much traction in the past. Adding them as pre-built views that get generated when the tasks list is created will certainly motivate users to utilize them and visualize their tasks better.

One more thing that's worth a mention here is the ability to create subtasks. If you look closely in the Timeline image above, you'll see a task called **VisualSP** that's indented. This is a subtask of the task that appears above it. The ability to break up large tasks into smaller chunks of work with subtasks is extremely helpful. The subtasks can then be assigned to various people and can be managed by themselves while still belonging to a major task item. This is a functionality that has been available in Microsoft Project for many years and now it has been manifested into the SharePoint tasks list.

The focus in the above section is on the task list. However, as stated earlier, there are other visual changes peppered around various SharePoint lists which would be worth exploring.

Searching within SharePoint Sites

Searching for information is of course an extremely important capability within the Intranet and Internet as a whole. We have become spoiled by being able to search for anything as it comes to our mind and expecting to find it immediately.

The whole search capability in SharePoint 2013 has been overhauled completely! Since the beginning of SharePoint 2001 until SharePoint 2010, we had two vastly different search experiences depending on the product that you had deployed. If you had only the base SharePoint product (called SharePoint Foundation in SharePoint 2010), you got the privilege to search only within the site collection. Then if you decided to move up to SharePoint Server, your options increased and now you were able to search throughout site collections in your whole farm. Generally, companies have multiple site collections deployed in their environment - definitely the right thing to do - so we're saying that if you wanted your people to search across those site collections, you had to shell out for SharePoint Server licenses. A further upgrade to another product that Microsoft provided, called FAST search, gave you even more capability and let you use search refiners, preview thumbnails of documents from search results and just overall made things better and faster.

The good news is that you get all of that good stuff still, but without the complexities of having to figure out which licensing you need for what type of functionality. There is no separate FAST search engine or other server specific search capabilities that had made things ambiguous and made everyone's heads spin in the past. It is all just 'SharePoint Search'. Period. When you deploy SharePoint (even just the base product SharePoint Foundation), you get all that SharePoint search has to offer in SharePoint 2013 out-of-the-box! A big and bold step from the SharePoint team to move in a wonderful direction of excellent search capabilities.

Since we are focused on power users here and search configuration still remains to be very much an IT Professional topic, our focus is going to be what is new and noteworthy searching within site collections, sites and within lists and libraries.

In SharePoint 2013, when searching for information within the site, data is extracted from the metadata of the items and presented as refiners on the quick launch to filter through search results: Result type, Author, Modified date and more.

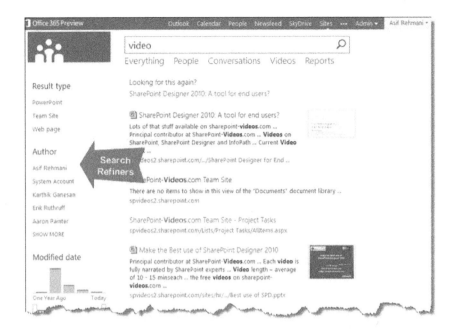

Search refiners

Search within a library or list stays in that library. It doesn't take you to another interface with potentially different branding (SharePoint 2010 shows you search results in an Application Layouts based page which has different branding applied to it). This might seem like a small thing, but not switching screen context after search is performed makes it a lot more efficient and easier to digest for the end user who is actually utilizing this functionality.

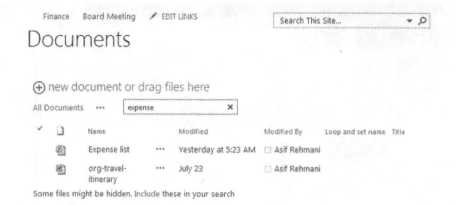

Search results within library

People Search

We are not only searching for information or data always. Many times we search for actual People within the organization. In SharePoint 2013, you can find a broader range of "experts" based on documents they've authored. Also, there are social connections that are presented in the query results. Meaning, when you hover over a person's name in the search result, a pop-up dialog appears showing you if/how you have any connections to that person as shown in the image below.

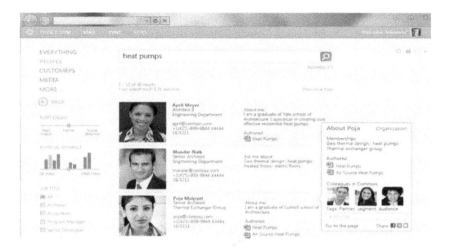

People Search

Search Driven Navigation

The traditional ways of thinking about search is also changing. Usually, the act of searching for something on the web or intranet involves going to the search box and typing in your search term. This is still true of course, but there is more to it. In the beginning of the world wide web, searching for data meant literally navigating through the handful of public sites available to find the information that you were looking for. It remained this way until the query search functionality got to the point where we stopped bookmarking sites and just started querying for everything that was needed at the moment on the fly - especially because a page that was compiled by someone in the past becomes stale too quickly. Information grows ever so quickly and the stuff compiled on the page becomes irrelevant. Well, not so much anymore... there is a better way!

Imagine navigating to a page which shows you all the latest and greatest data around a particular topic or subject area that you are interested in. This data would always be dynamic, up to date and never get stale. How's that possible you ask? Well, with pre-defined search queries implemented on the page of course. Instead of having a human compile all the information around a subject area at one point in time and letting it get outdated, the pre-defined search query runs automatically when you navigate to a page effectively providing you search driven navigation for your area of interest. The image below shows the *Shared with me* view of a MySite which is completely search driven and always brings back the latest results of which documents have been shared with me.

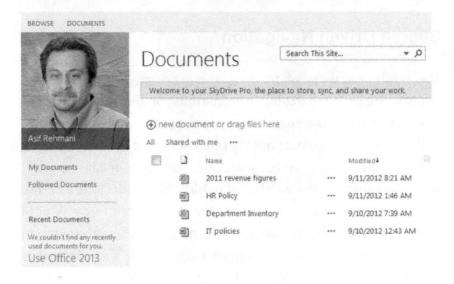

Search driven navigation

SharePoint 2013 gets very Social

What Is 'Social'... really? Well, it's the way we share and consume comments, feedback, thoughts and things interesting to us. We do it in the 'real world' and now quite a bit in 'cyberspace'. The online tools that facilitate the social paradigm are all around us of course. With the proliferation of Facebook, Twitter, LinkedIn and others, it's hard to get away from being Social online (although many have succeeded in ignoring this phenomenon altogether :-)).

Let's shift gears now to talking about what's new in the Social space within SharePoint 2013. The answer is A Lot! However, before I start running through the many things that you should look out for, please remember that to participate in social features, you need to have a MySite! That's correct. MySites need to be turned on and configured for any of the things listed below to work. Why? Well, because a lot of the features of social in SharePoint 2013 manifest themselves in a MySite. For example, you would navigate to your MySite to see the activities related to you and the people you are 'following' (a new social feature discussed below). That's just one of the many examples. More on this a bit later.

The Community Site

The Team Site template in SharePoint has been doing a great job for many years of providing a platform for groups of people to collaborate. Usually, a team site is centered around documents, calendars and tasks. That's at least the usual use of it. There are of course many other types of lists and libraries available in the team site template as well, but there usage usually gets sidelined and is not the main focus of the site.

One of the types of lists available in a team site template is Discussion Board. It's a nifty list to create and start holding newsgroup-style discussions directly on the team site. It works fairly well actually. However, you can't really extend the discussion board to do much more than just holding threads of discussions. Your question at this time might be: Well, what would I want it to do? To answer that for yourself, think of a real discussion board online. What can you do in that discussion board? Let's visualize some concrete examples such as the TechNet or StackExchange forums (just to name a couple of popular forum services online).

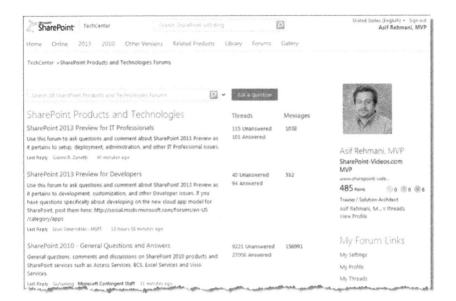

Microsoft TechNet forum

These forums let you feel part of the community when you are participating in them. Your real reward of course then is to have the satisfaction of knowing that you have helped someone by answering their question or providing thought-provoking feedback. However, in addition to that satisfaction, you can also earn points and badges. You can support a forum thread by Liking it or Voting for it. You can even make sure that you partake in future discussions of a specific thread by setting an alert on it or by "following" it so you get the notification of any additions or changes to the discussion.

There is a new site template that ships with SharePoint 2013 and it's called the Community site template. It hopes to provide a similar type of experience in-house as the online forum sites. This site template can be utilized to make a subsite in an existing site collection or you can use that as the top level site of a new site collection. Utilizing this template, you can build a community to discuss topics of common interest. Security management for this site works the same way as any other SharePoint site. Authorization can be inherited from the parent site or inheritance can be broken and you can manage the users directly at the site level. The discussion board and the threads within it are of course the main focal point of this site. To support the discussion, many features exist on that site template such as:

- A list of categories to classify each post
- A way to Like a post
- Members earn reputation points
- Ability to earn badges on the site

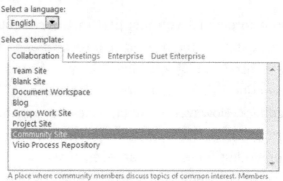

Community Site template

Let's look at some of this functionality in further detail.

Once again, keep in mind that the Discussion list is the main focus of the community site. The activities within this list and around it are what we are going to talk about.

The sidekick to the Discussion list is the Categories list. The categories list can be populated with the various categories that the posts would be relevant to. When creating a new post, you can choose a category to tag that post with. This would serve as a very convenient way to later discover relevant content by exploring the available categories on the community site.

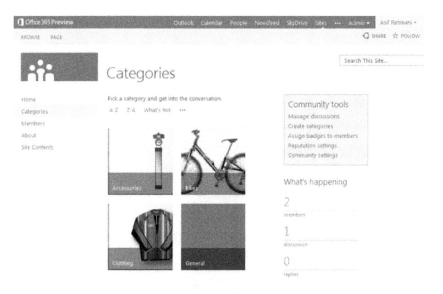

Community site discussion categories

Like it

When reading something we really like or agree with, many folks generally tend to provide comments, feedback or a general 'Thumbs Up' or a 'nod' to the author. The general accepted thumbs up or nod is now the Like button/link in cyberspace made famous by Facebook. Microsoft also adopted this functionality by providing a way to like a post in the community site. The way it works is that when you come upon a post that you like, you can click the Like link that appears directly below the post. The ramifcations of that Like are the following: Your newsfeed on your MySite will show that you have liked some content and the author's newsfeed will also show that you have liked her content. The like functionality is enabled and turned on by default. However, the site owner has the ability to change the like functionality to a rating system with the ratings from 1 to 5 stars if that works better for the members of the site.

Liking content, replying to content and other activities within the community site will earn you what's referred to as reputation points. Your reputation automatically starts building on the site as soon as you join it and start interacting with it. These reputation points then translate into badges that you will start seeing next to your name as it appears on that site. Earning these points and badges builds your reputation on this site. Every community site has its own system and your points and badges are not carried across multiple sites.

Badges can be earned and/or assigned by the community site owner (also referred to as the Moderator of the site). The assigned badges are also referred to as the gifted badges and they certify you as an expert on the subject matter.

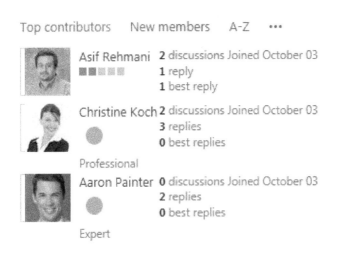

Community Members ⓘ

Top contributors   New members   A-Z   •••

	Asif Rehmani ■■■■■	2 discussions Joined October 03 1 reply 1 best reply
	Christine Koch ● Professional	2 discussions Joined October 03 3 replies 0 best replies
	Aaron Painter ● Expert	0 discussions Joined October 03 2 replies 0 best replies

Badges and points

MySites

MySites are required to be configured and running in order for people in the company to take part in other social aspects of SharePoint 2013 (such as the Community site described in the earlier section).

MySites generally look and feel the same. However, more features have been added on to it.

The Newsfeed functionality that appears when you enter a MySite contains all activity around the user. It is used to store user generated activities (the microblog posts) and also system generated activities (such as notification of change to a document you are 'following', activities regarding your 'liking' a certain item on a site, etc.). This feed looks and behaves very much like the feed in popular internet social media sites.

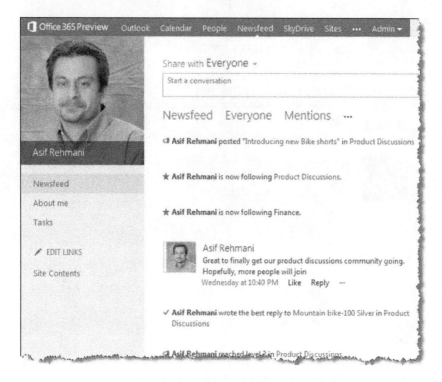

Personal Newsfeed

When you want to keep track of something specific, whether it be a person, site, document or a tag, you can 'follow' it. The way it's accomplished is by either looking for the word follow or a star icon around the object you want to follow. Then you simply click on either one of those things and now you are following that item. When you follow an object, any changes to the object or anything changed by that object shows up as activity in your newsfeed.

Following a person

The 'follow' functionality does not replace the alerts functionality. Alerts are still alive and well in SharePoint 2013 and work the same way as they did in SharePoint 2010.

Very much like Twitter, you can tag a post by using the hash mark symbol (such as #SharePoint). The intended result is the same as Twitter. You can have trending tags that are popular for the day. For example, if a new Chief Financial Officer (CFO) is joining the company and everyone is talking about it, they might all place the hash tag #CFO in their posts. So in turn, the #CFO tag will be the latest trend that will automatically get picked up and shown to everyone on their MySites. It's kind of like a news flash that's being produced because everyone is 'digging' it (pardon the pun here). Overall, a very nice-to-have functionality.

@Mentions view

Tagging a person or mentioning them gets their attention. People who use Twitter regularly know the power of how that works to get someone in the conversation. The same type of functionality is now available in SharePoint 2013. You can mention someone in a microblogging post that you are creating. So for example, let's say you wanted to say that Andrew was doing a great job, you would put the following in your microblogging post:

Great job @Andrew Connell for all of the information you share with the community

The @ sign is the key to making the mentions. As soon as you the put the @ sign in your post and start typing in the first couple of characters of the person's name, the system helps you by providing you possible choices. You pick the appropriate person you want to mention and continue typing the remainder of your post.

If and when a person gets mentioned, their Mentions feed view (available through the MySite's Newsfeed) shows all of their mentions as displayed in the figure below. In additions, as soon as someone mentions you, you get a notification through email as well so you can always keep abreast of the conversations involving you.

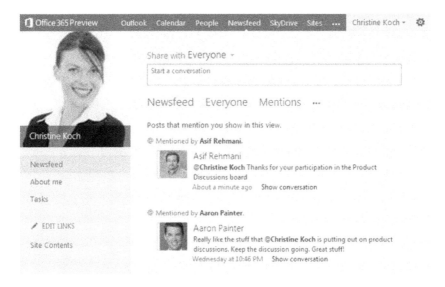

The Mentions view

Mybrary

The Documents library that appears at your MySite is also sometimes referred to as the Mybrary (as in My Library). This is the library that the MySite owner controls and uses to create, share, and collaborate on documents. It's just one single library as opposed to the two (Personal Documents and Shared Documents) we had in SharePoint 2010. The reason for the change: manageability by the individuals. So now, instead of putting documents in two different libraries (and potentially having duplicated documents in both), a user can just have a single copy of the document in one library that they can choose to keep private or share with others by assigning the appropriate permissions. A view of the Mybrary is shown in the image below. A complete discussion of this library is included in the Managing Documents chapter of this book. Please refer to that for further details regarding this functionality.

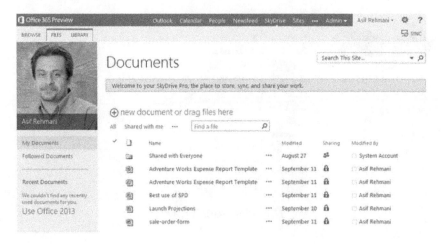

The main personal Documents library (Mybrary)

My Tasks

The ability to see all of my tasks information (and I mean all) has been a highly coveted functionality for a long time. SharePoint 2013 brings us the My Tasks view accessed through the MySite. The potential power of this search driven view is to provide the ability to have a single, aggregated view of all the task for the user across not just SharePoint sites, but also Microsoft Project sites as well as Exchange. This super aggregation is accomplished through a new service application called Work Management (WM).

The WM service app uses a hidden list in the user's personal site to cache all the aggregated data. Users can also create personal tasks that get stored in that list as well. A view of the My Tasks is shown in the image below.

A service application is instantiated and configured by the SharePoint Server Administrator. Since this book is mainly targeted towards Power Users. We will not be digging any further into the details of the Work Management service.

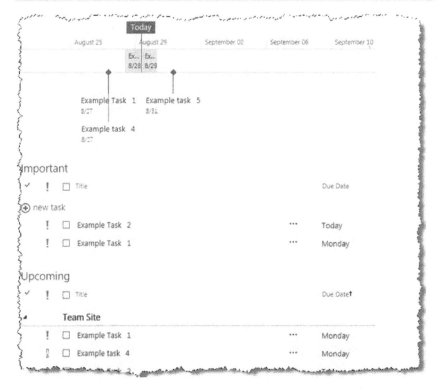

The My Tasks view

The real cool part about this functionality is that you can not only view all of your tasks, but also have the ability to manage the tasks right there. Meaning, if you see a task in this list which originates at a team site you belong to, you can edit the task right there in the My Tasks view and it will sync the task changes back at the original location of the task.

Keep it going

This book is being released while SharePoint 2013 is still brand new. Some things might change by the time the released copy of SharePoint 2013 is available publicly. I tried my best to give you a good understanding of many of the things to come in this release. My focus has been the Power User but I hope that all users within the SharePoint ecosystem would get something out of this book.

There is a growing number of articles, blogs, <u>videos</u> and other resources on the web regarding SharePoint 2013. I would highly encourage you to continue your journey looking deeper into this release with a focus on how it affects your role in the SharePoint environment.

Best wishes, good luck and keep in touch!

- Asif

<u>SharePoint-Videos.com</u>
<u>asif@sharepointElearning.com</u>

Dedication, Acknowledgements and Author's Bio

Dedication

This book is dedicated to my lovely daughter Alina.

Acknowledgements

First of all, I would like to thank God for giving me the courage to embark on yet another book project. Even though this book is not that long, it took many countless hours of research and dedication to bring this first book on SharePoint 2013 to fruition. Throughout the process, the lovely faces of my wife, Anisa, and my kids, Armaan, Ayaan and Alina, kept motivating me to work harder and do better. I'm so very thankful to having all of them in my life.

I would also like to acknowledge and thank the whole SharePoint community. Throughout the decade that I have been entrenched in the community, I have met and learned from many talented individuals and have gained a lot from their perspectives. I am still learning every time I talk to my SharePoint peers or an overwhelmed 'SharePoitnt guy/girl' - whether it is over phone, email, in one of my training classes or at one of the dozen or so SharePoint conferences that take place around the world every year. These thought exchanges and influences have been highly inspirational and motivational to me and keeps me going to create more SharePoint educational material like this book. Thanks to you all!

Author's Bio

Asif has been training and consulting on SharePoint technologies since 2002. He is a<u>SharePoint Server MVP</u> and MCT. He is a principal contributor at <u>SharePoint-Videos.com</u> and provides in-person and online training through <u>Critical Path Training</u>.

Asif has written many SharePoint curricula, dozens of SharePoint articles and authored books "<u>Professional SharePoint Designer 2007</u>", "<u>Beginning SharePoint Designer 2010</u>" and "<u>Real World SharePoint 2010</u>" by Wiley publications . He has produced hundreds of video tutorials on SharePoint. They are available at Microsoft <u>TechNet</u>, <u>MSDN</u>, <u>Channel 9</u>, <u>Office.com</u>, <u>YouTube</u> and <u>SharePoint-Videos.com</u>.

Asif has been a speaker at conferences since 2006 on SharePoint topics. He has presented around the world at numerous conferences including Microsoft's <u>TechEd</u>, <u>SharePoint Conference</u>, <u>SPTechCon</u>, <u>SharePoint Connections</u>, <u>SharePoint Fest</u>, <u>Best Practices Conference</u>, <u>SharePoint Saturdays</u>, SharePoint Roadshows and more.

Asif was the co-founder and is currently one of the leaders of the <u>Chicago SharePoint User Group</u>.

For further information, please visit <u>http://www.sharepoint-videos.com/about</u>